To David, Christian, Fiorella and all my friends that are always supporting me in all my new adventures.

To all the people who are facing changes and who have the courage to start a transformation for the better by taking control of their own lives.

It's never too late to start again.
Start now
and go where you want to go!
—— ..

CHANGE. CREATE. TRANSFORM.

START NOW

A 21-Day Workbook
For Transforming Your Life

MOIRA BUZZOLANI

ISBN: 979-12-210-5271-8

MBUZZ Consulting & Coaching

www.moirabuzzolani.com

Illustration & Concept Design by: Moira Buzzolani
Copywriting by: Jamie Black
Book Graphic by: Abdul Rehman

This is my *Workbook*

. . . .

MY NAME IS

TABLE OF CONTENTS

Introduction

The objective of this book is to provide a straightforward and effective guide for individuals seeking to enhance their lives. It offers a three-week journey that aims to bring clarity to one's current context and define the initial steps necessary to reach desired destinations.

During times of difficulty or change, confusion can arise. The crux of the matter becomes the crucial first step in determining the right direction and where to begin.

It is never too late to regain control of one's life and start living differently. I penned this "operational diary" during a challenging phase in my own life that I persevered through.

"Change always starts with a first step."

The diary serves as a practical booklet. It's where you can jot down ideas, thoughts, and feelings. It is best to follow the path chronologically since the proposed sequence is optimal for achieving the ultimate goal: self-awareness, understanding one's current position and envisioning future aspirations.

Navigating the entire journey without a guide or a supportive coach may prove challenging at times. While embarking on this independent journey, I urge you to maintain discipline while approaching this experience as a voyage of personal growth that will yield significant benefits if undertaken with commitment and the right mindset. Flexibility and adaptability are a vital part of redefining one's life. Embrace this operational tool with a sense of playfulness and view it as an opportunity to discover more about yourself and perceive situations from a fresh perspective. Be curious, open-minded, and determined, as wondrous things can happen.

Wishing you an enjoyable and fruitful journey through this book!

Week One

01

It Starts Here: 21 Minutes For You

Start here: Allocate a minimum of 21 minutes for yourself every day. Make note of this commitment in your calendar, diary, smartphone alarm. The means doesn't matter as long as you document this appointment with yourself. Highlight it, ensuring it's visible throughout your day.

These 21 minutes signify more than just a time slot; they represent a genuine declaration of intent: a personal commitment to enhance your life. This dedicated time for yourself signifies your desire for self-improvement and serves as a starting point.

"Improving your life is a choice, you can make it now!"

If you have picked up this book, chances are you are currently in a place where you are ready to explore something new. Perhaps you find yourself in a period of intense stress or a sense of emptiness, or you simply realize that you can no longer manage your life as you once did. Something has stirred within you, urging you to take action. Rest assured; you are on the right path. You are here.

Do not feel compelled to make drastic changes; sometimes, it is the small things that yield significant benefits. Together, we will embark on a journey to discover a fresh approach to addressing your past, present, and future.

True transformations stem from within. It's crucial to cultivate a different, more functional way of thinking to serve as a foundation for establishing a new course of action. We will diligently work on both aspects of thought and action.

"Big or small, changes always start with the first step!"

So, what should you do during these initial 21 minutes of self-devotion?

First and foremost, remind yourself that you are worthy of this time and that the moments you dedicate to redefining your life are genuinely invaluable, both for yourself and for those around you. Often, we claim to lack time, but in reality, we fail to make time. It is not something that happens to us passively; rather, it is a conscious decision we make.

Approach this journey with the firm belief that "you are deserving of this time and that dedicating ourselves to improving our lives is time well-spent." This mindset will propel you forward and enable you to persist on this path, even when faced with obstacles or moments that trigger thoughts like: "it's not worth it," "it's too exhausting," "it's all pointless," "I can't do it," or "I'm too tired." These self-sabotaging phrases may frequently arise in your mind, but rest assured, they are normal and experienced by everyone. The key to overcoming them is through repetition:

"I am worth it, and the time dedicated to improving my life is necessary time well spent."

Repeat this phrase several times and say it out loud. Hearing yourself say it with your ears (and not just in your mind) makes it more real and allows your thoughts to enter your subconscious faster. This is why it is crucial that you repeat the same sentence several times. Don't tire yourself out right away and remember that you must keep doing it until you believe it completely.

The second important step during these first 21 minutes is to plan your week. Take a sheet of paper and divide it into seven parts. Then write down when you will take 21 minutes for yourself on each day of the week. You can also use the diagram at the end of the chapter.

The important thing is to set aside this time for yourself (and only for yourself) during a moment when you know you are calm. The end or beginning of the day is usually the easiest time, but it depends on your habits and preferences. Also, put a checkbox at the end of each day, and when you have dedicated the 21 minutes to yourself, mark the box with "done!"

"The 21 minutes for you are the first step towards a better life. Every time negative thoughts sabotage you by telling you to let it go, tell yourself that it's worth it!"

☐ **MONDAY**

From: ....

To: ....

☐ **TUESDAY**

From: ....

To: ....

☐ **WEDNESDAY**

From: ....

To: ....

☐ **THURSDAY**

From: ....

To: ....

☐ **FRIDAY**

From: ....

To: ....

☐ **SATURDAY**

From: ....

To: ....

☐ **SUNDAY**

From: ....

To: ....

02

My Achievements

Today is dedicated to cultivating awareness of the positive actions you have taken in your life, in order to nurture your self-confidence. Self-confidence plays a vital role in propelling you forward and attaining positive goals in your present and future, so it is crucial to prioritize it.

You will examine your past and delve into your personal history, allowing you to fully acknowledge all that you have accomplished so far. Surely, there have been both triumphs and setbacks: moments when you excelled and instances when things didn't go quite as planned. However, there are valuable lessons to be learned from both experiences.

Life is a continuous learning process, and whether circumstances are aligned with your expectations or veered off in unexpected directions, what truly matters is how you perceive and interpret them through a constructive lens.

One important notion to keep in mind is that "there are no mistakes, only feedback." This means that even if a situation does not unfold as desired, it does not signify failure; it simply indicates that, "for the time being," things are not unfolding as envisioned.

 *"You only fail when you stop trying."*

From even the direst situations there is always an opportunity to take valuable lessons. These experiences not only teach us what actions to avoid in the future but also guide us in developing more constructive ways of responding to adversity.

I understand that it can be challenging to adopt this perspective, especially when tough events unfold. However, viewing them as "temporary" and as "opportunities for personal growth" will enable you to extract the maximum benefit from whatever comes your way.

This ability to perceive situations as transitory is a key factor in achieving personal success. By recognizing that circumstances are impermanent and embracing them as chances for improvement, you empower yourself to navigate through challenges with resilience and grace.

"When you think that it didn't go the way you wanted, how hard it is, how difficult it is, remember that it is a temporary phase."

We must rely on the passage of time, recognizing that its subtle workings can eventually bring forth a glimmer of hope. The timeframe for this transformation varies greatly – it may take weeks, months, or even years. There is no universal rule that applies to everyone.

Nevertheless, one certainty remains: despite the passage of time and the diverse adversities faced, there always lies the opportunity to start again. I have witnessed individuals emerge from the depths of the most unimaginable circumstances and, against all odds, accomplish remarkable achievements that inform their lives in tremendous ways.

"I don't know how long it will take, but one day life will smile again."

What steps can you take right now to become aware of the beautiful things that life has offered you so far? Below, take a moment to freely and intuitively write down all the positive experiences and accomplishments from your past. Allow your thoughts to flow without excessive questioning. Aim for at least twenty experiences.

These entries may encompass professional achievements, such as securing a desired job, receiving an accolade, aiding a colleague in need, obtaining certification in a course, or liberating yourself from a toxic work environment. On a personal level, victories might include celebrating a marriage, performing an impactful act of kindness for a close friend, caring for your parents, welcoming a child into your life, embarking on an independent living arrangement, dedicating time to exercise at the gym, liberating yourself from an unhappy relationship, or bravely embracing the end of a harmful partnership. These examples serve as a starting point, but it is now up to you to construct an extensive catalog of positive experiences!

"Learning to see the glass as half full will help you understand how to keep filling it."

This will be your achievement list, write it carefully!

List of My Achievements

Remember: It is crucial to list a minimum of twenty items, it's very important you understand the successes and achievements you have already reached in your life. If you require additional time to complete the list, take it. Remember that it is not solely significant events that should be included; small yet meaningful actions, undertaken with sincerity and compassion, hold equal importance.

"We can't always do big things in life, but we can do small things with great love."

~ Mother Teresa ~

Writing as many things as possible is of paramount importance as it brings you into the "stretching" phase. Think of it like going to the gym: if you neglect stretching, your muscles may indeed strengthen, but they won't attain the desired length, thus compromising your overall flexibility. We want to train the mind to embrace expansive possibilities at this moment.

By expanding your perspectives, you will unlock a greater abundance of solutions in the future — what I fondly refer to as the "creativity stretch." So, let your imagination roam freely and allow your list to flourish, for it is through this exercise that you nourish the seeds of ingenuity and embark upon a journey of limitless discovery. Let the creativity flow and stretch your mental horizons!

You can also use mind-mapping for this exercise. It is up to you to select a tool that can help you to create an extensive list. Do not forget the goal "list as many achievements as possible".

Now that the list stands compiled, take a moment to read it aloud attentively. As the next step, schedule a dedicated session for tomorrow, marking it as the second phase of this exercise.

Remember to mark day two on your weekly plan as completed — don't forget to tick it off. Well done!

03

The line of success

Here we are on Day 3, are you ready to begin the next exercise? Today we will be doing an exercise called "The Line of Success," which will complement what you did on Day 2. Completing this exercise with awareness and attention, it will help improve your mood and see yourself in the right perspective.

To start, take a piece of paper and draw a timeline on it (you can attach multiple sheets together to create a longer timeline). Ensure that you have enough space to write without feeling restricted.

Using the achievement list you compiled yesterday, plot the various accomplishments on the timeline. The first dot on the left will represent the earliest positive result you obtained, and the last dot on the right will be the most recent result. Please refer to the example below:

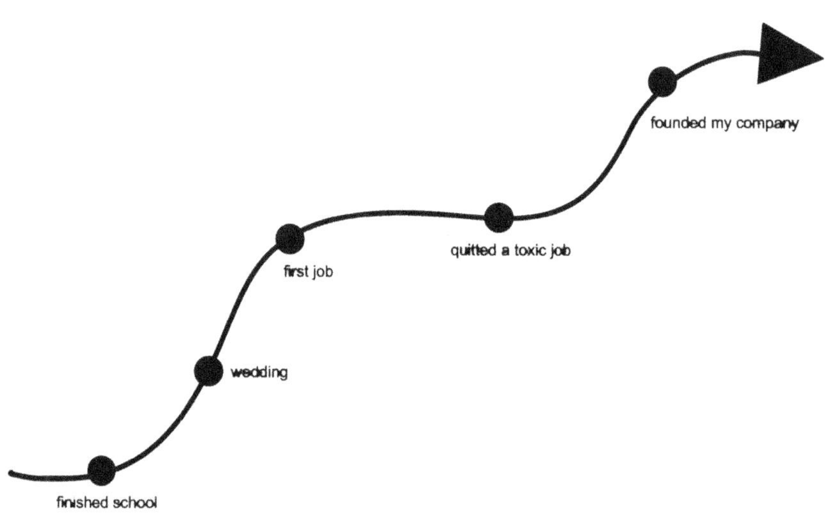

You can enhance your experience by using colored pencils to draw your line in a creative and expressive manner. Let your imagination run wild and create a line that is unique to you. It can be linear, curved, or even go up and down. There are no limits or rules here – just let your artistic intuition guide you. Remember, this exercise is meant to be enjoyable and celebratory, as it serves as a visual representation of all the positive things you have accomplished so far.

If you find that 21 minutes is not enough and you need more time to complete this exercise, feel free to allocate an extra day or an additional quarter of an hour solely for this purpose.

Remember, you have full control over how much time you allocate to activities, so take as much time as you need. Now, let's dive in and create your own vibrant and dynamic line of successes!

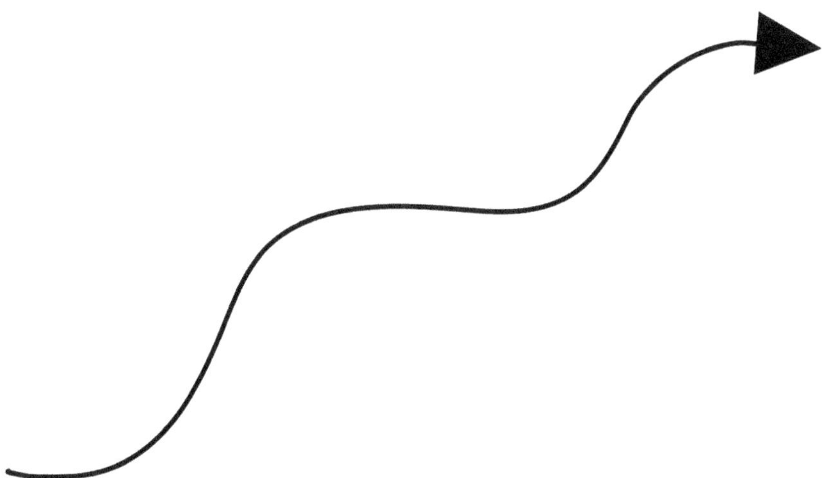

Now, keep your list nearby for this journey as it will serve as a powerful reminder of all the positive and courageous actions you have taken.

When revisiting and reflecting on your list, you may find a mix of genuine successes and what I like to call "false failures."

Let me clarify this distinction for you. Sometimes, there are events that may not initially appear as successes, but upon closer examination, they prove to be crucial in achieving something extremely positive.

Allow me to provide an example to illustrate this concept. Let's say one of the items on your list is "quitting a toxic job." At first, this may not seem like a triumphant achievement. It might have been a challenging and painful journey and the act of resigning may not have felt like an immediate victory. In retrospect however, that difficult decision to leave turned out to be one of the most positive choices you've ever made. It opened doors to new opportunities such as finding a better job, pursuing further education, or embracing a healthier lifestyle.

These events that initially appear as setbacks but lead to beneficial outcomes are what I refer to as "false failures." They are situations that despite their initial difficulty or unhappiness, have brought you significant benefits.

If you haven't included any "false failures" on your list, I encourage you to reflect on past experiences and identify situations that may have seemed negative initially but ultimately led to excellent results and surprising outcomes. Take some time to think about and add these instances to your list before moving on to Day 4 . This exercise will further expand your perspective and acknowledge the hidden achievements within perceived setbacks.

FALSE FAILURES

Negative Event	Positive Twist

Well done. You have successfully transformed those "false failures" into positive outcomes.

It's important to remember that the inherent positivity or negativity of events is not just determined by the events themselves. The key factor lies in your interpretation and your capacity to place them within the broader context of your life.

Never forget that you have accomplished numerous things in your life, and that means you are fully capable of achieving even more in the future. Keep this belief alive and let it fuel your motivation and determination. You have what it takes to succeed once again.

"There was a moment when you craved something you didn't have. And now you have it. Believe again because you can achieve all your goals."

04

Relationships

Welcome to Day 4 of your journey! We will now delve into the topic of relationships. As you may already know, the connections we have with others, as well as with ourselves are crucial elements in attaining what we refer to as "happiness." Many studies have demonstrated that healthy relationships and a supportive environment are key to leading a fulfilling life.

In today's world, what we now call a "network" is essential not just for our professional endeavors but also for our daily, social interactions.

For this exercise, we will focus on the individuals who play a significant part in your life. We will begin by creating a list of all the people you regularly interact with. They could be family members, colleagues, sports or leisure activity partners, old friends with whom you occasionally communicate, neighbors, and so on.

Take a look at the grid in the next page and fill in the first two columns by writing down the names and roles of these individuals. By role, I mean what they represent to you – whether they are friends, colleagues, teammates, and so on. Once you have completed the list, move to the third column on the right and indicate the impact they typically have on your mood. If they are supportive individuals who bring positive vibes or thoughts into your life, simply write "positive." On the other hand, if they tend to focus on the negative aspects of things or drain your energy, write "negative." If you find it difficult to decide, you can use the term "neutral."

However, try to limit the use of "neutral" as it signifies that the person's presence does not significantly influence your life one way or another.

Think of it like a mathematical equation: adding zero to a number does not alter its value. Zero lacks the power to bring about any change. Here's an example to illustrate this concept.

People	Role	Impact
Giulia	Friend	Positive
Frank	Colleague	Neutral
Nicholas	Brother	Negative

Now it's your turn. Use the structure below.

MY NETWORK

People	Role	Impact

Count how many negative, positive, and neutral people you have in your circle of regular interactions. Write below how many there are and who they are.

Positive impact:

Nagative impact:

Impact neutral:

Now that you have completed the exercise, to get an even clearer picture of who can really help you get through the difficult moments and who will tend to make the situation even more gloomy, you can write the names of the people listed above in this space:

NEGATIVE

POSITIVE

NEUTRAL

Reducing interactions with people who have a negative impact on your energy is crucial, especially when you are feeling down. It may not always be possible to completely avoid such individuals, but being aware of their non-positive impact can help you approach them with clarity and objectivity.

"People's opinion is always based on their experiences and not yours. Listen to everyone and treasure it, but then do what's right for you."

I would like to emphasize an important distinction before moving forward: positive people are not necessarily those who always agree with us and negative people are not necessarily those who hold different opinions. True friends may have differing viewpoints, but they express them with respect for who we are. These individuals can offer valuable insights and different perspectives on a situation. On the other hand, there are people who may appear open, sunny, and carefree, but their constant complaining and focus on their own troubles make us feel bad or inadequate. They drain our energy and leave us exhausted after every encounter.

I'm not suggesting that we should avoid people who are in need or seeking support. It's crucial to be mindful of not allowing "energy vampires" to steal your energy. Selecting the people we interact with consciously and not allowing ourselves to be overwhelmed by the opinions (and negative vibes) of others is extremely important during this phase of self-discovery.

In times of difficulty, we are more sensitive and vulnerable. Protecting ourselves and choosing those who will support us on our journey without holding us back is a wise decision. There is no reason to feel guilty about prioritizing our well-being and surrounding ourselves with positive influences.

"Choosing to meet and discuss with those who help us recharge is the pure wisdom of those who know how to climb the most difficult mountains."

Based on my experience of over a decade in a multicultural environment, I have learned that different countries and cultures have distinct ways of giving and receiving feedback. What may be appreciated as direct and straightforward in one culture could be seen as harsh or inappropriate in another. It's essential to consider the background of the person you are communicating with and evaluate their comments (as well as your own) based on their cultural perspective, values and behaviors.

The activity of categorizing people as positive, negative, or neutral is simply a way of taking a "snapshot" of your current relationships. It is not meant to accuse or pass judgment on anyone's intentions.

Instead, it serves as a quick and practical way to understand:

- ▶▶ Those who can offer you a different perspective

- ▶▶ Those who can provide support and help recharge your energy

- ▶▶ Those individuals who tend to drain your energy or consistently view situations in a negative light.

"Exchanging opinions and points of view is always the best way to contextualize the situation and gain a more comprehensive understanding of what we are experiencing."

Having people who are vastly different from each other in our circle of acquaintances is incredibly valuable. Diversity serves as an extraordinary gift of diverse perspectives allowing us to develop a comprehensive understanding of our surroundings. Others often observe events in a way that may elude us, and multiculturalism aids in expanding our horizons and envisioning fresh possibilities when we are open to it. Being receptive to alternative interpretations of events is immensely enriching.

"It is much easier to see situations from the outside and that is why having friends is really like having a precious treasure."

Have you ever tried the colored cube exercise? Imagine a cube with different colors on each side, resting on the ground. When a group of people sits around the cube in a circle, each person can only see the top and one or two sides. No one can see the side on the ground or the one opposite to them. If you ask participants to describe the cube based on what they see, you'll likely receive different responses. One person may say, "The top is yellow, and the two sides are blue and red," while another person on the opposite side might say, "The top is yellow, and the two sides are orange and green." Are they lying? Certainly not. They are simply perceiving the same object from different perspectives.

The same principle applies to personal matters. Having people who can see and interpret situations differently from us can provide a clearer understanding of what is happening.

Now it's time to take action and engage with those who support you and can enrich your viewpoint. Pick up the phone and start a conversation with the first person on your list.

Don't isolate yourself or be hesitant. Embrace the exploration of different perspectives. You can even choose to interact with someone you've categorized as "neutral" or "negative," but be mindful that their influence may be demotivating. The choice and assessment are yours.

It's time to utilize your valuable network as a source to broaden your horizons and take proactive steps forward!

The Inner Dialogue

Have you ever engaged in self-talk? Perhaps in front of a mirror or while driving? On what occasions do you find yourself doing it? Are you concerned about it, or do you feel comfortable talking to yourself?

Different individuals have varying preferences when it comes to solitude. Some people constantly seek company and activities, while others require silence and individual pursuits to recharge and find peace.

The way we connect with ourselves is not a one-size-fits-all solution that brings peace and calm universally.

Considering this:

- Where do you stand on this spectrum?
- Do you find solace in your own company, or does being alone make everything more challenging?
- How do you converse with yourself when in the presence of others?
- Have you ever pondered over these questions?

A first step is to acknowledge that we engage in an ongoing internal dialogue, both when alone and in the presence of others. Have you ever paused to consider this phenomenon? It's known as "inner dialogue" and plays a crucial role in maintaining our emotional equilibrium and personal growth.

We must first ask ourselves:

Are you aware of how you interact with yourself?

How do yuo speak to yourself? What tone do you use?

Is the voice you hear always your own or does it sometimes resemble the one of others?

What characteristics does this inner voice possess?

Rest assured; these experiences are completely normal — everyone goes through them!

Recognizing and understanding our internal thought processes is an activity that fully deserves our attention.

One day, I stumbled upon a thought in a book that was truly enlightening:

"Wisdom is the ability to eliminate thoughts that weaken you."

This thought resonated with me so deeply that I wrote it down on a note and placed it on my bathroom mirror, ensuring I would see it every morning upon waking up. That note remains in the same spot to this day.

I used to believe that speaking to myself in a serious and authoritative manner was the right approach. I thought that being hard on myself would make me stronger and more determined, enabling me to achieve what I desired. It was like an internal game between a strict teacher and an inexperienced student.

This particular quote completely transformed my perspective. It compelled me to reflect on the significance of choosing thoughts that empower us rather than demoralize us. The change wasn't easy, but I began to ease up on myself, making space for kindness and understanding. As a result, I started to improve, and the results started to manifest.

I came to realize that wisdom lies in selecting thoughts that strengthen rather than weaken us. I understood that being determined and focused on a goal doesn't entail pushing ourselves to the extreme and sacrificing everything and everyone. It means taking care of ourselves and creating conditions for a sustainable and enduring journey, much like a marathon. Life is not a linear race; it is an unpredictable and diverse path. Knowing how to allocate our energy is a fundamental aspect of the game.

The way we speak to ourselves varies significantly from person to person and is influenced by our upbringing, the individuals we've encountered, and our experiences.

Changing our inner dialogue, if necessary, is one of the most challenging endeavors because it occurs automatically and unconsciously. Nonetheless, consciously exploring what is genuinely beneficial to us and what is not is a worthwhile pursuit.

Now consider some possible past situations. Read the following examples and answer.

Example 1: When you received a poor grade in school, what echoed in your mind? "I'm so stupid!" or "I should have put in more effort; I'm intelligent, but I didn't apply myself enough" or "I know the material; it's the professor who lacks understanding."

How did you react to these events?

Example 2: When you expressed interest in someone, and they declined, what did your internal dialogue sound like? "I'm not interesting enough; that's why they rejected me" or "They said no because they like me and want me to pursue them further" or "If they say no, it's because they lack intelligence. I don't date unintelligent individuals."

Example 3: When someone gives you a compliment, how do you respond internally? Do you tell yourself, "Of course, I'm so charming that they couldn't help but notice me" or "They said that out of courtesy, even if it's not true" or "How strange, a compliment. What do they want from me? What's the hidden agenda?"

"It is not what happens in itself, but how it is interpreted that makes the difference."

In order to change our behaviors and reactions, we need to take the first step and understand how we talk to ourselves. Only later, once we understand our patterns, can we decide to keep the thoughts that help us and change those that weaken us.

All clear? Well, let's go!

Exercise:

The exercise that I am proposing is to be completed back-to-back on Days 5 and 6. Its purpose is to give you the opportunity to increase awareness of the thoughts and stories you tell yourself.

Throughout both days keep a sheet handy (or carry this diary with you).

Pay attention to the way you talk to yourself. Simply write down your thoughts in the first column on the left.

Example:

Phrase	Effectiveness	Reframing
I'm really stupid, I got the test wrong.	Weakens	I'm smart, I have to study differently next time to get the test right
I'm good, even if the class test didn't go as I wanted. Next time I will study more.	Strengthens	-

You don't have to fill out all the fields at once. The key is to jot down your internal thoughts in the left column. Once you've completed the list, you can assess whether these statements have a positive or negative impact on you. In the right column, you can then rephrase the disempowering sentences to make them positive and constructive. If a sentence is already motivating on its own, you can leave it as is or, if you prefer, rephrase it to make it even clearer and more impactful.

Choosing empowering phrases that enhance our self-image is particularly beneficial during times of discouragement or sadness.

Phrase	Effectiveness	Reframing

Phrase	Effectiveness	Reframing

Here are some basic rules to keep in mind:

1. Avoid using negative adjectives to describe yourself. Saying phrases like "I'm stupid," "I didn't understand anything," or "I'm incompetent" doesn't help at all. It is crucial to always affirm your self-worth (remember the phrase repeated several times on Day 1?). This means using positive adjectives to describe yourself, such as "I'm intelligent," "I'm a good person," "I'm reliable," and so on. Repeat affirmations to yourself that have a positive impact within you. Maybe we've been accustomed to hearing something different, but that is a problem with whoever said those things, not the truth. We must treat ourselves well because we deserve it.

    However, this doesn't mean constantly telling ourselves that we're always great or perfect, even when we make mistakes. It means being gentle with ourselves and genuinely seeking constructive ways to improve.

2. We are not defined by our behaviors. Having gifts and talents doesn't exempt us from making mistakes or poor choices. That's why it's important to separate our sense of self from our behaviors or the results we obtain. For example: "I am an intelligent person, but I acted foolishly when I insulted my colleague." Distinguishing who we are from our actions is vital for building the self-confidence we deserve. It's a matter of practice and learning how to do it in a functional way.

Here's a suggested structure to use:

▸▸ "I am a (positive trait/adjective)____person,

   but I acted ________________________________(description of the negative behavior).

Repeat this structure for different situations:

▸▸ "I am a (positive trait/adjective)____person,

   but I acted ________________________________(description of the negative behavior).

▶▶ "I am a (positive trait/adjective)_______________________________________person,

but I acted _______________________________________ (description of the negative behavior).

▶▶ "I am a (positive trait/adjective)_______________________________________person,

but I acted _______________________________________ (description of the negative behavior).

▶▶ "I am a (positive trait/adjective)_______________________________________person,

but I acted _______________________________________ (description of the negative behavior).

▶▶ "I am a (positive trait/adjective)_______________________________________person,

but I acted _______________________________________ (description of the negative behavior).

▶▶ "I am a (positive trait/adjective)_______________________________________person,

but I acted _______________________________________ (description of the negative behavior).

▶▶ "I am a (positive trait/adjective)_______________________________________person,

but I acted _______________________________________ (description of the negative behavior).

▶▶ "I am a (positive trait/adjective)_______________________________________person,

but I acted _______________________________________ (description of the negative behavior).

▶▶ "I am a (positive trait/adjective)_______________________________________person,

but I acted _______________________________________ (description of the negative behavior).

▶▶ "I am a (positive trait/adjective)_______________________________________person,

but I acted _______________________________________ (description of the negative behavior).

Continue this pattern for each situation you want to reframe.

By following these guidelines, you can gradually shift your mindset and develop more effective behaviors. Remember, it takes practice, but learning to reframe your thoughts is the key to feeling better and implementing positive changes. This is equally valuable regardless of context, whether personally or in professional settings as well.

07

An Overview

Here we are at the end of the first week. I hope you didn't forget to check off all the items on your weekly plan. Enjoy that satisfaction!

Today, take 21 minutes for yourself to reflect on what you have accomplished during the past six days. Review the exercises you completed, revisit anything that needs a bit more attention and contemplate what you have learned:

1. Value yourself.

2. Acknowledge your successes.

3. Recognize the people who uplift you and those who drain your energy.

4. Pay attention to your self-talk and maintain a positive inner dialogue.

Use this time today to allow what benefits you to settle and flourish even more. Research indicates that self-esteem is often undermined by recurring negative thoughts. That's why doing the exercises once is not enough for a shift in your thinking to occur. To develop new patterns, repetition is necessary.

I'll leave some space for you to write your own reflections on the first week. You can consider the following questions as helpful prompts to get started:

▶▶ What did I enjoy doing the most during the 21 minutes for myself?

▶▶ What was most beneficial to me?

▶▶ Have I noticed any improvements in how I perceive myself?

▶▶ Have I become more aware of how I communicate with myself? How do I engage in self-talk?

▶▶ Was it helpful for me to speak with one or more "supporters"?

▶▶ What was particularly challenging for me to do? Why?

Take your time to reflect and jot down your thoughts. This self-reflection will contribute to your personal growth and progress.

Before proceeding to the second week, remember to create your "twenty one minutes for yourself" plan, just like you did on the first day of this journey. However, this time, you will add something special: a reward for yourself, and make sure to write it down.

If you have reached the end of the first phase of the program, it means that you are doing an excellent job and you are truly committed to improving your life! Celebrate your progress and acknowledge your determination.

"You deserve an award for your exceptional commitment, it's not something that everyone can achieve!"

It can be a tangible reward such as fresh flowers for your kitchen, a pair of shoes you have had your eye on, or as simple as grabbing your favorite chocolate or ice cream as a treat. At the same time, it can be an experience that holds significance for you, such as a gym membership, a visit with a close friend, or an appointment at the hairdresser. The important thing is that it carries personal meaning and brings you joy!

☐ **MONDAY**

From: ....
To: ....

☐ **TUESDAY**

From: ....
To: ....

☐ **WEDNESDAY**

From: ....
To: ....

☐ **THURSDAY**

From: ....
To: ....

☐ **FRIDAY**

From: ....
To: ....

☐ **SATURDAY**

From: ....
To: ....

☐ **SUNDAY**

From: ....
To: ....

At the end of the second week, I will give myself the following reward:

45

Week Two

08

Beliefs

Do you know what beliefs are? They are simply thoughts or ideas that we hold to be true. Beliefs give meaning to our actions, events, and behaviors and they are the focus of today's exercise.

For instance, let's consider the belief that "If you study, you will have more opportunities to find a well-paid job." This belief influences the decisions we make for ourselves or our children, guiding us towards a certain direction.

On the other hand, you may hold the opposite belief that "Studying is useless, and it's better to gain practical work experience." In this case, your decisions would likely differ from those who hold the first belief.

It's important to note that there is no right or wrong belief. However, what we believe to be true significantly impacts our actions and choices.

Beliefs can be categorized into two types: empowering beliefs and limiting beliefs. It's crucial to be aware of how these beliefs affect us.

"Limiting beliefs" can hinder our ability to find solutions, recognize opportunities and even restrict our daily actions. This can make us feel stuck or trapped, like sinking in quicksand.

"The "empowering beliefs" are those that help you overcome blocks and difficulties making you even stronger and more determined than before."

Often, we are unaware of holding these dysfunctional beliefs; we simply assign meanings to events or situations automatically. The choice of which meanings to attribute is not always conscious. They seem to descend upon us as if from above. Many of these beliefs have been "taught" to us or subtly passed down, with varying levels of awareness.

Allow me to provide another example. How frequently have you caught yourself uttering phrases such as, "Wealth only brings problems" or "Money doesn't bring happiness"? Such beliefs can severely limit your financial well-being, as they condition you to view opportunities for improving your financial status as unworthy pursuits. Essentially, you may convince yourself that it is better not to strive for wealth, fearing the accompanying money-related issues. This can act as a form of self-sabotage in a way. We can be very good at talking ourselves out of things!

While these beliefs are not inherently true, they may have been ingrained in you by the environment in which you were raised. Perhaps your parents, teachers, or influential figures close to you instilled them. At times, such beliefs are shared by entire groups or societies. Additionally, you may have formed personal beliefs based on your own experiences or specific outcomes you observed following particular events.

The origin of your beliefs is immaterial; what truly matters is your awareness of them.

"The question you need to ask yourself now is: is it useful for me to think this way in order to get what I want?"

If your answer is "no," you can dive deeper into understanding your beliefs by asking yourself additional questions:

1. Who said it?

2. Who taught you that belief?

3. Is it always valid? Does it hold true as an absolute rule for everyone and in all situations?

4. Can you find examples of individuals who have achieved different outcomes? For instance, do you know someone who, despite attaining wealth, has experienced positive improvements in their life?

"Your beliefs aren't based on universal laws that always apply, which means you can change them when they don't help you get where you want to go."

You may not have the power to change what others think, but you have the ability to change your own beliefs and make them "empowering". For instance, instead of believing "Wealth doesn't buy happiness," you can reframe it as "Wealth, when used wisely, can bring positive outcomes for myself and those around me in various situations." This shift in belief can help you view situations that bring financial benefits in a positive light rather than a negative one.

Let me provide you with another example of how beliefs can impact success in the workplace. Consider the belief, "If you don't go to university, you will never have a good job." This belief can be positive or negative depending on your desired goals. If your aspiration is to become a lawyer, then education and attending university are undoubtedly crucial. However, if your chosen path does not necessarily require a university degree, holding onto the same conviction can be highly limiting. The definition of "a good job" varies from person to person, and there are many individuals who find happiness and fulfillment in careers that don't necessitate a university education.

Allow me to share a story about two dear friends, Anna and Romeo, who have contrasting perspectives. Anna has secured a "good job" at a prestigious company, but whenever an opportunity for promotion arises, she refrains from pursuing it due to a fear of inadequacy. Despite not having completed her university education, Anna possesses all the qualities necessary to succeed. Her belief that a university degree is an absolute requirement limits her confidence in attaining her desired position and adversely affects her performance in job interviews.

On the other hand, Romeo enrolled in university but found the classes extremely tedious. He started applying for various jobs even before graduating. Eventually, he landed a position in a leading company within his field of interest. At a certain point, Romeo decided to withdraw from his studies and pursue alternative learning methods independently. He consistently maintained the belief that practical experience was paramount to achieving his goals and that if he desired a degree, he could pursue it in his spare time. After a couple of years, Romeo became a team lead in an IT services company and is currently content and fulfilled.

These two individuals exemplify completely different approaches to the university experience. The beliefs they hold have profoundly influenced their respective outlooks on the future. There is no definitive right or wrong answer. It depends on what you aspire to achieve and how you perceive situations. Being aware of your limiting thoughts and knowing how to rephrase them can genuinely transform your mindset and, consequently, your approach to various circumstances. Are you conscious of your limiting thoughts? Do you know how to reframe them?

I want to emphasize that the purpose of this example is not to imply that studying is futile or that attending university is wrong. On the contrary, I firmly believe in the value of higher education as an opportunity. I advocate against limiting people's potential based solely on one factor.

Below, I propose an exercise that can assist you in reframing unhelpful thoughts.

Exercise:

Begin by writing down the limiting thought that you recognize as obstructing your progress (the thought that hinders your goals).

Examples may include:

- "I'm too old to pursue this,"
- "Employers only hire individuals with prior experience,"
- "Competitions are highly challenging and accept only a few applicants,"
- "Due to the economic crisis, I will never find a job,"
- "You need connections to secure employment," and so on.

Identify the limiting thought that holds you back and reframe it into a positive statement that motivates you to take action.

Reframing of limiting thoughts

Limiting Thought

There is the crisis that I will never find a job.

Reframing

There is a crisis, and it is very difficult to find a job now, but there are some cases where it happened and I could be one of those cases.

Limiting Thought

Reframing

Limiting Thought

Reframing

Limiting Thought

Reframing

At the end of this chapter, I'll leave you with a "reinforcing" thought that you should never forget:

"If you have thoughts that are limiting you, remember that you have the power to change them and transform them into your allies that can help you achieve your goals."

By reframing negative thoughts into positive ones and focusing on taking action towards what you want, you can create a mindset that empowers you to overcome challenges and achieve success. It may take time and effort to shift your perspective, but with practice and persistence, you can cultivate a positive and empowering mindset that will serve you well in all areas of your life.

09

DAY

Values

Let's take a moment to check-in. How are you feeling? Are you experiencing any confusion or a decrease in enthusiasm, or are things becoming clearer and you're eagerly looking forward to continuing your journey?

If you're feeling a bit drained, don't worry, it's completely normal and can happen during the process of making changes. Remember, transformations don't occur overnight; they require time and consistency.

Keep in mind that the key is not to execute all the exercises perfectly, but rather to consistently engage in them and to review and revisit what you have written and learned. This is about staying committed.

The journey towards positive change takes time and effort.

"Repetition is the key to turning actions into habits. The same goes for thoughts. Do you want reinforcing thoughts? Repeat them, repeat them, repeat them."

As each day passes, we keep building. Another important thing to explore that makes up this puzzle we are exploring together is your values.

Values serve as guiding principles in life, representing what you believe in. Some values remain constant, while others may evolve and shift as we journey through life.

Even our priorities can change and adapt over time. This is a natural part of our growth and development, as we are never exactly the same as we were before (even though at times it may feel that way). We continually evolve and transform, whether consciously or unconsciously.

"Values are like a compass of life, if you don't look at them and observe them consciously you risk going off course."

In different moments in life values can then drastically change. Here is an example. There may come a time in life when career and professional success take precedence. You may find yourself relocating to a new city or dedicating long hours to secure a promotion or desired job. However, at some point, a shift occurs, and the longing for exploration and freedom emerges. You may take a sabbatical, embark on travels, and seek diverse experiences without being overly concerned about your current job. Then, one day, the desire for starting a family takes center stage, and the allure of travel and absolute freedom wanes. You devote yourself to your partner and begin planning a future together, which may involve children, a home, and a settled location.

Life evolves, and so do we. Our priorities shift in accordance with our personal growth, and this is completely natural. It's crucial to recognize how our needs change and to respond accordingly, as failing to do so can have significant consequences. Being in alignment with oneself is not something to be taken for granted, as it enables us to live a life with minimal regrets, or perhaps even without any regrets at all.

"Deciding with full awareness what is important to us (now) is the key to alignment with ourselves."

Now, I present to you a simple exercise that will help you discern the values that currently guide your life. This exercise is a classic coaching technique and can be repeated periodically whenever you feel the need to realign with yourself.

Exercise:

Below is a list of values. Take your time to read through each one, and feel free to add any additional values that you believe are missing from the list.

List of values

- Adventure
- Altruism
- Authenticity
- Awareness
- Beauty
- Candies
- Career
- Carefree
- Change
- Collaboration
- Compassion
- Consistency
- Courage
- Creativity
- Curiosity
- Decisiveness
- Decisiveness
- Dignity
- Diversity
- Dynamicity
- Economic Welfare
- Efficiency
- Environment
- Ethics
- Family
- Fidelity
- Freedom
- Friendship
- Fun
- Future
- Generosity
- Goodness
- Gratitude
- Harmony
- Health
- Honesty
- Honor
- Hope
- Humility
- Imagination
- Inclusion
- Independence
- Integrity
- Intelligence
- Intuition
- Joy
- Kindness
- Leadership
- Life
- Love
- Loyalty
- Luxury
- Nature
- Novelty
- Optimism
- Order
- Pardon
- Patience
- Patriotism
- Peace
- Perseverance
- Personal Growth
- Physical Well-Being
- Recognition
- Reliability
- Respect
- Responsibility
- Safety
- Sense Of Humor
- Serenity
- Simplicity
- Size
- Spirituality
- Spontaneity
- Sport
- Struggle
- Success
- Time
- Tradition
- Trust
- Truth
- Utility
- Visibility
- Vulnerability
- Wealth
- Wedding Ring
- Wisdom
- Work

Now write below the ten values that you consider important in this phase of your life:

My 10 Most Important Values

1.   2.

3.   4.

5.   6.

7.   8.

9.   10.

Now it gets harder, you only must choose five, write them here:

My 5 Most Important Values

1.   2.

3.   4.

5.

Now is the time to write down your top three guiding values.

My 3 Most Important Values

1.   2.

3.

Understanding our motivations and what propels us in life is highly impactful when faced with important decisions. Recognizing that life encompasses various stages and how our values can shift in terms of importance over time empowers us to make more accurate and well-informed choices.

"If you want to be satisfied, make sure you are aligned with your values. If you know what's important to you, making the right choices will become easier and you'll feel less frustration when everything isn't perfect."

10

D A Y

Interpretations

Have you ever considered that different individuals can take away different meanings to the same word or concept?

During a workshop, I asked twenty participants to draw a flower on a small piece of paper within a few minutes. It was a simple and straightforward task. Each person depicted a flower based on their own mental image. When finished, the participants took turns pinning their sketches to the wall. The result was a vibrant display of various types of flowers in different sizes and colors - a true kaleidoscope of a garden.

If such a simple task produced so many different outcomes, imagine the complexity that arises when dealing with more intricate concepts, like the ones we have explored together so far!

Let us look at an example that we can all most likely draw from in one way or another: the concept of family. Family is a universal concept present in nearly all societies, both ancient and contemporary. The way it is understood and lived can vary considerably. If family is one of your guiding values, how do you embody it? How do you act and communicate? I am referring to concrete actions and practical behaviors. How do you fully experience this value? These are the questions I'd like you to reflect upon.

One of my clients, whom I will refer to as Paola, shared during our meetings: "Family is of utmost importance to me, which is why I take care of household chores, do the shopping, and cook for my husband and children. I thoroughly enjoy telling my children bedtime stories to ensure they sleep peacefully."

Let's observe how Paola translates the value of family into practical actions (based on her statements):

- Taking care of the house
- Grocery shopping
- Cooking for the family
- Telling her children bedtime stories every day

On the other hand, another client, Isabella (also a fictional name), responded to the same question as follows: "I work extensively, putting in long hours as I have my own company. My objective is to provide my family with a dignified life. I enroll my children in one of the city's top schools where they can learn languages, play tennis and soccer twice a week. Sports are beneficial. I ensure they consume only organic food as health is paramount. The highlight of my week is spending quality time with them on weekends."

Here is how Isabella translates "giving value to the family" into practical actions:

- Enrolling her children in one of the city's top schools to learn languages
- Encouraging her kids to participate in sports (soccer and tennis)
- Ensuring her children consume only high-quality, organic food
- Engaging in playtime with her children during her free time
- Working to maintain a good standard of living for the family

This example demonstrates how the same value can be interpreted and translated into completely different actions.

"There is not just one way of living our values, the important thing is that what we do makes sense to us."

Exercise:

It's time for you to identify your own guiding values. Write down your top three values and then list concrete actions that you will take to make them a reality.

Value 1

To bring it to life, I will:

Value 2

To bring it to life, I will:

Value 3

To bring it to life, I will:

Reflection:

How are you feeling? Was it straightforward to translate your values into concrete actions?

I hope this exercise provides you with a tool to contemplate how and what you need to do to achieve what is important to you. I also hope it has been beneficial for you to realize that everything you do is driven by a profound force within you.

11

DAY

Gratitude

Gratitude is a powerful emotion that can move mountains! There are books, studies, and research dedicated to showcasing and celebrating the power of gratitude. It's a unique feeling because it allows us to appreciate what we have and often take for granted. Gratitude helps us to gain perspective and focus on the positive things in our lives, which in turn makes us feel good.

It's natural to become accustomed to everything and to pay more attention to the negative aspects of life rather than the positive ones. Sometimes we don't even see the beautiful things in our lives anymore because we have been conditioned to value what we possess automatically. Often, it's only when we lose something (a person, a benefit, a job, an object, etc.) that we realize how important it was to us. Have you experienced this as well?

Related to gratitude is the idea of being present in the moment (mindfulness). That means being able to notice what we have and what's in front of us. Paying attention is an important part of gratitude and it requires conscious effort.

"Attention is essential in everyday life. Not only because it brings us to the "here and now", but also because it allows us to appreciate life, feel better and reduce the anxiety that sometimes strikes us without warning.

Exercise:

I would like to invite you to think about yourself. The first part of the exercise is very simple and forms the foundation of self-awareness.

Begin by observing yourself from an external perspective, as if you were looking at yourself from the outside.

Take a few moments to observe and reflect on:

What do you see?

What are you doing?

How do you speak?

How do you appear?

What are you saying?

Write down any thought that comes to mind.

Now, I would like you to make a list of your current skills and talents. Don't hesitate to acknowledge and appreciate your own abilities. You don't have to be humble in this exercise. Just think about all the wonderful qualities you possess.

While humility is a valuable trait, I don't want it to limit you from expressing positive aspects about yourself. Allow yourself the freedom to acknowledge and celebrate who you are and what you are good at in this exercise.

Imagine that you are promoting a product and you need to list all the positive and admirable qualities and features it possesses.

That product is you!

My skills and talents

What you have done just now has been an example of cultivating gratitude for oneself.

Write "THANK YOU" below as a sign of gratitude for being who you are.

My Thanks for who I am

12

"The Thank you" game

Now that you've become aware of how lucky you are to be who you are, it's essential to give thanks also for the precious things you have in your life: people, situations, opportunities, objects.

Every night before bedtime, my eight-year-old son and I play the "thank you game." We take turns expressing something we are happy and grateful for out loud. Children are particularly adept at this and often share words filled with wisdom. My son frequently expresses gratitude for "the sun," "the cozy bed," "a little friend" he played with during the day, or even "Christmas" (even in August!). These things don't have to be grand, but rather meaningful to you, and the gratitude should come from deep within!

Now, I invite you to proceed with the exercise. You will now create a list of "things" you are grateful for. Allow this list to be compiled spontaneously without overthinking. Write down whatever comes to mind, without attaching judgment to each item. There are no items that are more or less important; there are only things that hold value to you.

Thanks for:

Now, It is crucial for you to read these two lists every night before you go to bed and as you drift off to sleep.

You can also choose to write them down on your phone, take a picture, or jot them on a piece of paper to keep in your pocket, so you can access them in a way that easiest for you.

Whenever you have a pause or a moment when you're not feeling positive, take them out and read them! Over time, your natural inclination to feel grateful will soar, and positive things will manifest in your life. I assure you!

13

Emotions and Change

would like to begin today with a few words about emotions, and the transformative power they hold. There are numerous wonderful books on this subject, but I won't delve into complex theories here. My aim is to encourage you to reflect on your emotional experiences so that you can navigate and manage different emotions in a more natural and anxiety-free manner.

There are sensations that bring you joy and others that cause you pain. It is important to understand that both serve a significant purpose. Emotions can be seen as a genuine compass, revealing what is transpiring within us and guiding us towards the right direction—or away from the wrong one.

When something brings you pleasure, you naturally seek to repeat it. That said, when something causes discomfort, you instinctively try to avoid it. There are times when recurring patterns, instead of improving our well-being, lead us into negative situations. These mental patterns are learned and sometimes persist because we are unaware of them. They rest in our subconscious. Other times, we may be aware of them but still find ourselves replicating those patterns. It's the equivalent to having an autopilot that takes us not only where we want to go but also where we don't want to go!

The capacity to change these patterns does exist. Change typically induces discomfort in almost everyone. As creatures of habit, humans often prefer to stay where they are, even if they are not entirely content, simply because it is familiar. Disrupting the status quo always brings discomfort and sometimes even fear. People decide to change only when two extreme conditions are met:

1. The current situation has become so painful and intolerable that they are compelled to change it.

2. An enticing opportunity presents itself, tempting them to change in pursuit of something more appealing and fulfilling.

In both cases, something significant needs to occur — either negatively or positively — to spark this energy for change.

But what if no external factors intervene to provide such energy and willingness to change? The risk is that one remains stuck for years without making any progress. If you are unhappy with your current circumstances but struggle to find the strength or motivation to move forward and change your situation, there is one question you can ask yourself: What would need to happen for you to take the first step towards change?

"Imagine what should happen. The power of imagination makes miraculous things happen!"

Exercise:

Take a moment to contemplate what circumstances, whether positive or negative, would need to occur for you to initiate a change. Below, list the possibilities without concerning yourself with their feasibility.

Now, write down the "positive" scenarios that would prompt you to alter your current situation:

The list of "positive" levers of the change

Now is the time to write down the "negative" situations or events that should happen to push you to change the current situation:

The list of "negative" levers of the change

Reflection:

▸▸ Was it challenging to create the two lists?

▸▸ Did you include more positive things or negative things? These lists will be valuable to you as they can help you determine whether you are inclined to 1) avoid things that don't make you feel good or 2) pursue positive goals.

If you have listed an equal number of items in both lists, it indicates that both negative and highly positive aspects have an influence on your decision-making towards change. However, there is a risk of becoming stuck in a middle ground, leading to stagnation.

Reflecting on these two lists is crucial not only to gain self-awareness but also to leverage the positive or negative aspects based on what you deem most beneficial for achieving change and attaining your desired outcomes. Having the ability to influence the direction of your drive for change is incredibly valuable.

14

DAY

The Bigger Picture

Today´s focus will be on exploring the diversity of areas that shape your life by considering your situation in a holistic manner.

Every person's life is a tapestry woven with various threads, including relationships, family dynamics, work or study commitments, leisure activities, physical and mental well-being, personal growth, financial circumstances, and more. These aspects contribute to the overall fabric of your life.

Exercise:

To initiate this activity, I invite you to use the a diagram on the next page. Within this diagram, assess and assign a score from zero to ten to each area of your life. Use a cross or a dot to indicate your evaluation on the corresponding lines. Once you have completed this assessment, combine the points to gain an overview of your scores. Take note of the areas that received the lowest and highest ratings.

Allow the example below to guide you in making your own assessment of your current situation. Take your time and reflect upon each area thoughtfully. This exercise will provide valuable insights into the areas that require attention or improvement, as well as those in which you are thriving.

LIFE THERMOMETER

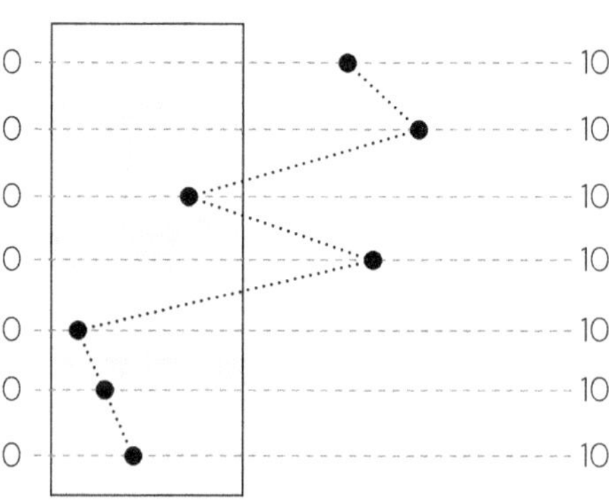

Lowest ranked domains:

1. Physical and mental health
2. Spirituality/mission
3. Personal growth and development
4. Surrounding environment

Now you can do the exercise along the lines of the example.

LIFE THERMOMETER

Domain	0											10
Leisure and entertainment	O	O	O	O	O	O	O	O	O	O	O	
Financial situation	O	O	O	O	O	O	O	O	O	O	O	
Physical and mental health	O	O	O	O	O	O	O	O	O	O	O	
Family and personal relationships	O	O	O	O	O	O	O	O	O	O	O	
Personal growth and development	O	O	O	O	O	O	O	O	O	O	O	
Spirituality and mission	O	O	O	O	O	O	O	O	O	O	O	
Surrounding environment	O	O	O	O	O	O	O	O	O	O	O	

Lowest ranked domains:

1. ....

2. ....

3. ....

4. ....

Reflection:

▸ How are you feeling after assessing your current situation?

▸ Does the overall picture align with your initial expectations?

▸ Were there any unexpected surprises or revelations?

Take a moment to reflect on the results and consider the areas that require your attention in order to cultivate a sense of well-being within yourself and in your relationships with others.

I recommend focusing on the four aspects that received the lowest scores in your assessment. By prioritizing these areas, you can begin to identify specific areas for improvement. Referencing the example below, address the aspect ranked number one as the most urgent, followed by number two, and so on.

01. **Physical & Mental Health**   02. **Spirituality & Mission**

03. **Personal Growth & Development**   04. **Surrounding Environment**

Remember that this exercise is an opportunity for self-reflection and growth. By acknowledging and working on these aspects, you can enhance your overall satisfaction and establish a more fulfilling existence for yourself and those around you.

Use the "viewfinder" shown below and write in the four areas you want to focus on.

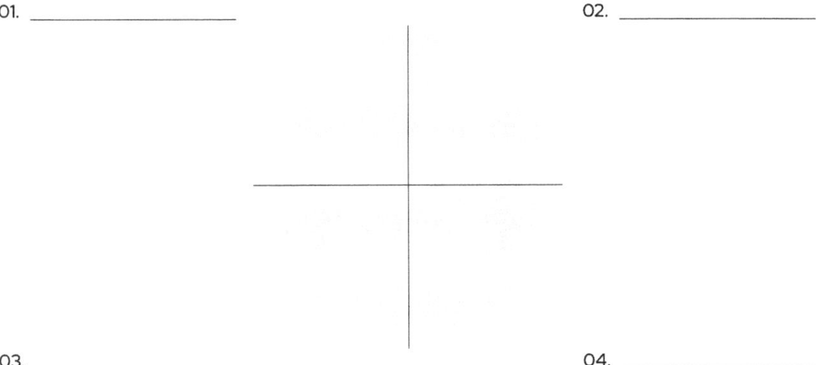

01. ______________________   02. ______________________

03. ______________________   04. ______________________

For each area, write now what is positive and negative in each of your life. A simple list of what you "see" right now. A sort of "written photograph".

Negative and positive things in the area 1:

Positive   Negative

Negative and positive things in the area 2:

Positive   Negative

Negative and positive things in the area 3:

Positive   Negative

Negative and positive things in the area 4:

Positive   Negative

The purpose of this chapter was to reflect on the things that are already working and on the things that need to be improved in some areas of your life. Remember, these lists are generated from the areas you have identified as priorities for yourself.

 *"Awareness is the first step towards improvement. "*

Now take a breath. You did a great job! How do you feel now?

Remember to tick all the boxes of the second week plan and don't forget to give yourself the gift you promised.

Be proud of yourself, it's not easy to do what you're doing with courage, determination and will.

Week Three

15-16-17

D A Y

Define Goals!

To start Week 3 we have bundled together the next 3 days. They will be intense as you will be asked to take a magnifying glass and figure out what you want and how to leverage the foundational work you have put in place over the last 14 days for what's next.

First, don't forget to make the "21 minutes for me" plan. It's the last week of our growth journey and it's worth not giving up right now.

> *"Step by step you climb the mountains."*

☐ **MONDAY**
From: ....
To: ....

☐ **TUESDAY**
From: ....
To: ....

☐ **WEDNESDAY**
From: ....
To: ....

☐ **THURSDAY**
From: ....
To: ....

☐ **FRIDAY**
From: ....
To: ....

☐ **SATURDAY**
From: ....
To: ....

☐ **SUNDAY**
From: ....
To: ....

At the end of the third week, I will give myself the following reward:

When it comes to goal setting, I find a metaphor to be highly effective. Imagine your mind as a satellite navigator: if you focus on where you don't want to go, the navigator will lead you nowhere! If you input the name of a state or country, the navigator will take you to that general area, but the destination remains broad. It is only when you provide specific details like the street name, house number, postcode, and city that the navigator can lead you exactly where you want to go.

Similarly, with your mind, the clearer and more specific your goals are, the easier it will be to navigate and reach your desired destination.

"The mind is like a navigator: the more precise you are, the faster you will get where you want to go."

There are various strategies to effectively define goals, and one such approach is called "The Seven Steps."

The first step is to clarify what "YOU" truly want, not what others want for you, but what you desire for yourself. Having a clear vision of your own desires is crucial, so take your time, and if needed, more than 21 minutes.

Exercise Day 15:

Begin by closing your eyes (yes, actually do it) and envision yourself in an ideal situation, as if you were watching a movie.

Don't impose too many limits on yourself because often the obstacles appear larger in our minds than they are in reality. Imagine yourself as both the director and the lead actor of the movie. Remove any unwanted elements from the scene. Engage in this exercise without restricting yourself excessively or placing numerous obstacles in front of your dreams.

You don't have to write down impossible dreams, but rather set goals that are enticing! Goals that make you believe your life can improve, that already make you feel happier and more fulfilled. Start by simply observing how you feel when you think about your ideal life. Imagine it vividly.

Exercise Day 16:

After allowing your thoughts to wander for a while, grab a pen and paper and get to work—put it all down in black and white!

When writing your goals, it's important to follow some basic rules that I have summarized below. Your goals should:

1. **Be positive:** Express your goals in positive terms and describe the exact end result you wish to achieve. Write them without using negation. What does this mean? Instead of writing, "I don't want to weigh 64 kg anymore," write "I weigh 60 kg."

   (Always focus on the result you desire rather than what you don't want to happen. Write your goal in the present tense, imagining that you have already achieved it.)

2. **Be inspiring:** Formulate a goal that is filled with positive energy and makes you feel good. Visualize it as if it's already accomplished and consider how wonderful it will be once you reach it. Simply stating, "I want to weigh 60 kg" may not ignite excitement about your goal. Instead, writing, "I weigh 60 kg and

I feel fit and energized," will immediately connect you with the reasons behind your goal and evoke feelings of achievement.

3. **Have a timeframe:** Define a specific deadline for achieving your goal. Having a well-defined time frame helps you stay focused and effective in pursuing what you want. It prevents you from endlessly postponing action and keeps you committed to the desired outcome.

4. **Be within your influence:** Set a goal that you have full or at least partial control over. It's essential that you can influence the result or have a significant impact on it. There may be situations beyond your control that cannot be changed, and in such cases, acceptance is necessary.

Once you have established a goal to achieve, you can start listing at least seven concrete actions that can help you reach it. The seven-step outline is simply a list of seven activities that contribute to achieving your desired outcome.

Here's an example:

Scope 1	Health
Objective	I weigh 60 kg and feel in perfect shape and full of energy. I will make it by August 31st of this year. (Today is May 1st, I weigh 64 kg and I feel tired and tired)
Step 1	I join the gym and go at least twice a week
Step 2	I always and only use the stairs (not the elevator)
Step 3	I take my bike to work every day (even if it rains)
Step 4	I drink healthy and sugar-free drinks (herbal teas, water, orange juice, etc.)
Step 5	I include vegetables in my daily diet (carrots, zucchini, salad)
Step 6	I walk at least 30 minutes a day
Step 7	I eat healthy snacks that give me energy (apple, banana, kiwi)

Having listed seven actions that will aid in achieving your goal, you will maintain focus on what you can do to influence the desired outcome. This provides you with a clear direction to follow and identifies immediate steps to take. The order of the actions does not have to be chronological, and repetition can be included for increased effectiveness. The more precise and specific you are in defining the actions, the easier it will be to implement them.

There are no limitations to the seven steps. You can expand the list at any time if you feel the need to include additional actions that can assist you. Be cautious not to set the bar too high and risk feeling dissatisfied. The sense of well-being you experience by following your initial seven steps must remain constant and is crucial for your success. Allow yourself to feel accomplished and better each time you complete one of the seven steps.

It's important to clearly outline what you will do rather than what you will NOT do. Focusing on positive actions and behaviors enhances your ability to make progress and achieve your goals.

"The mind does not recognize negation, get used to thinking positively."

If I were to tell you "Don't think of a yellow elephant with pink dots," you would immediately envision an elephant with pink dots in your mind. This illustrates the power of instructions we give to our brains. It is crucial to always focus on what we want rather than what we don't want.

Now is the opportune moment to take action!

For each area you have identified earlier, write down a goal and the seven steps that will guide you towards its attainment.

Scope 1

Objective

Step 1

Step 2

Step 3

Step 4

Step 5

Step 6

Step 7

Scope 1

Objective

Step 1

Step 2

Step 3

Step 4

Step 5

Step 6

Step 7

Scope 1

Objective

   Step 1

   Step 2

   Step 3

   Step 4

   Step 5

   Step 6

   Step 7

Scope 1

Objective

   Step 1

   Step 2

   Step 3

   Step 4

   Step 5

   Step 6

   Step 7

Exercise Day 17:

It is time now to write down shortly why the 3 goals/scope are so important for you. Simply answer these questions:

How do you feel when you get them?

What changes will occur?

What positive things will happen?

Which impact on your life?

What is the impact on the life of others?

So far, you have accomplished the following:

1. Identified the areas in your life that you want to improve and visualized how you will feel like.

2. Defined your goals with precision and clarity and outline the initial seven steps to progress towards them.

3. Defined why they are so important to you, and which benefits they will bring to your life.

Congratulations! You are in a fantastic position. Now, over the next couple days it's time to reflect on a vital aspect: Happiness!

18

Happiness

would like to conclude this section with some reflections on a topic that resonates with everyone: happiness.

Happiness is a subject that has been extensively discussed, studied, and explored in various cultures by philosophers, gurus, and experts. Given its universal appeal, I believe it is important to dedicate a chapter of this journey to this concept.

After all, the pursuit of happiness is a fundamental aspiration shared by individuals across ages, educational backgrounds, professions, genders, and cultures.

When asked to make a wish or express their desires in life, many people often respond with a simple yet profound statement: "I want to be happy."

The purpose of this book is to assist you in enhancing your life and gaining clarity about how you want to navigate the future's possibilities and opportunities. At this stage, contemplating the meaning of happiness can be tremendously beneficial in this endeavor.

"Happiness is something that we all want to achieve and that we all deserve, without exception."

There are fundamental principles regarding happiness, which can be considered as guidelines for leading a happier life. I will present a few of them for contemplation:

1. **Embrace the present moment:** Focus not only on appreciating what you currently have but also on making decisions based on the information and circumstances at hand. By evaluating the present and listening to your inner voice, you will make conscious choices.

2. **Avoid judgment, both of yourself & others:** Judgment leads to dissatisfaction. There will always be those who possess more or less than you, so it's better to recognize that people have different stories, and refrain from judging them or yourself. Continuing to do so will lead to a state of constant unhappiness.

3. **Filter external opinions:** While it's valuable to listen to others and gain inspiration from different perspectives, it is essential to trust your own judgment. Pay attention to your inner voice and determine whether their suggestions align with your own needs and values.

4. **Cultivate gratitude:** Acknowledge and appreciate the talents and blessings in your life, understanding their true worth. Gratitude plays a significant role as it allows us to value what we have and fosters generosity in our actions. Being grateful and generous contributes to a positive and joyful mindset, giving deeper meaning to our lives.

5. **Maintain a light-hearted attitude:** Learning to give appropriate weight to situations helps cultivate happiness. Embrace a sense of lightness, enabling you to face what truly matters without magnifying or burdening yourself with what holds little importance.

6. **Foster faith:** Faith does not solely pertain to religious beliefs but encompasses a belief in positive outcomes. It is not about denying negative realities but rather maintaining a mindset that something positive will emerge from any circumstance. It is the conviction that "I believe in heaven even when I find myself in hell."

7. **Treat yourself with love and kindness:** Anticipate and exhibit love and kindness towards yourself. By doing so, you will demand and extend the same treatment to others. Kindness and a compassionate mindset will open doors, bring tranquility, and establish you as a person who enriches the lives of those around them. (Remember our Positive, Neutral, Negative exercise? How would you like to be described?)

8. **Gain perspective:** Take a step back and view situations from a broader perspective. Remember that appearances can often deceive. Dedicate time to focus on what truly matters, rather than getting lost in trivialities and details. By gaining distance and examining the bigger picture, you can attain a more comprehensive understanding of the situation.

Exercise:

Now, let's delve into the final exercise of this journey. Close your eyes and imagine yourself at the age of one hundred. Reflect on your life, recalling both the successes and the aspects that didn't align with your desires. Ponder on your victories, defeats, moments of redemption, and experiences of happiness or unhappiness. Then, imagine a young child entering the room, standing before you, and looking into your eyes. This child is you at the age of five or six. He gazes at you, curious, and ask:

- ▸▸ Reflecting on your life, what accomplishments fill you with pride?

- ▸▸ How would you like to be remembered?

- ▸▸ What valuable lessons have you learned in your life that you believe are crucial for leading a happy life?

- ▸▸ Share them with me so that I may learn and apply them to my own journey towards happiness.

Summarize below the suggestions you would give to your "younger self" to help them face the future life.

Tips for my "younger self"

1.

2.

3.

4.

5.

6.

7.

8.

9.

10.

This exercise can be extremely revealing. It focuses you on what really matters in your life. It makes you distance yourself from contingent situations and gives you a clearer perspective on what is worth and what is not.

"The current situation is just a phase; it won't last forever. Life is like a movie, it's worth looking back and sometimes forwarding the movie to see situations in perspective ".

Take the time to reflect on what is true for you and what has made you happy. After writing what your "old self" says to your "child self", take a break and dedicate yourself to the following exercise only tomorrow: The picture of happiness.

19

Picture of Happiness

To engage in today's activity centered around happiness, I recommend finding a secluded space and surrounding yourself with things that bring you joy and comfort.

Your focus will be on introspection, constructing an external perspective of yourself. In this visualization, you will envision yourself in a state of complete happiness. You are content and possess all the things that bring you joy and satisfaction.

By immersing yourself emotionally in this mental image, you will gain insights into the specific actions, both small and significant, that you need to undertake to reach your desired destination. Envision the image within you, considering the vibrant colors, delightful scents, and radiant light. Reflect on who accompanies you, the activities you engage in, your surroundings, and immerse yourself in the intricate details that define your state of absolute happiness. Allow your mind to form a vivid picture where everything you desire is easily accessible.

Once you have completed this mental journey, take the time to write down every aspect you visualized. Ask fundamental questions to yourself:

- What genuinely brings me happiness?
- What do I aspire to achieve?
- What experiences make me feel satisfied?
- Who do I want to surround myself with?
- How do I wish to feel?
- What are my individual desires, unique to me alone?
- What makes my life meaningful?
- What makes a fulfilling life?

Exercise:

My Picture of Happiness & Fulfilment

To make the exercise more effective, set aside some extra time to visualize your desired state of happiness. This will help you connect with what you truly want and provide a clear picture of your end goal. Consider creating a vision board to capture this image. You can make it physically using paper, glue, and photos, or digitally using a tool of your choice. Regardless of the means, visualization can be incredibly powerful tool to amplify what you are creating for yourself.

20

D A Y

Positive Thinking

We have reached the end of this journey together. You did it!

First, I want to say "congratulations"!

CONGRATULATIONS

Not everyone finds it easy to embark on a personal growth journey and see it through to the end. While it's common to start with enthusiasm, true progress requires not only persistence but also the ability to make substantial changes toward a new and more fulfilling life.

Not everything magically transforms at once, but I'm confident that something has changed and that a greater sense of awareness now resides within you. This awareness extends not only to where you want to go but also to your values and how to embody them.

The main purpose of the path outlined in this book is to encourage self-reflection: to explore our personal resources and determine how we can leverage them to achieve our desires. The exercises presented can be revisited cyclically and whenever we feel the need for clarity, alignment, and balance with our current state.

To conclude this "Diary", I would like to share some positive thoughts that can uplift you during challenging moments. It is crucial to think and repeat positive affirmations, especially when facing difficulties.

Our mind cannot differentiate between the real and the imaginary, so nurturing positive thoughts (that are also true to us) will automatically lead to a state of well-being. It may take time to fully experience this shift, so be patient, but it will happen.

Enjoy reading and remember that it's never too late to take control of your life and make improvements. We can all transform for the better!

Positive Thoughts and Beliefs

 *"Time spent improving your life is valuable and well spent."*

"You can always improve, and you can always start over."

"There is always a solution even when it seems there isn't."

"Even when you don't understand it, things happen for a reason and time will show you that."

"Life is made up of phases: there are happy and easy moments, and complicated and difficult moments. Thinking that everything must always go the way you want is the basis of unhappiness, because it's impossible for that to happen."

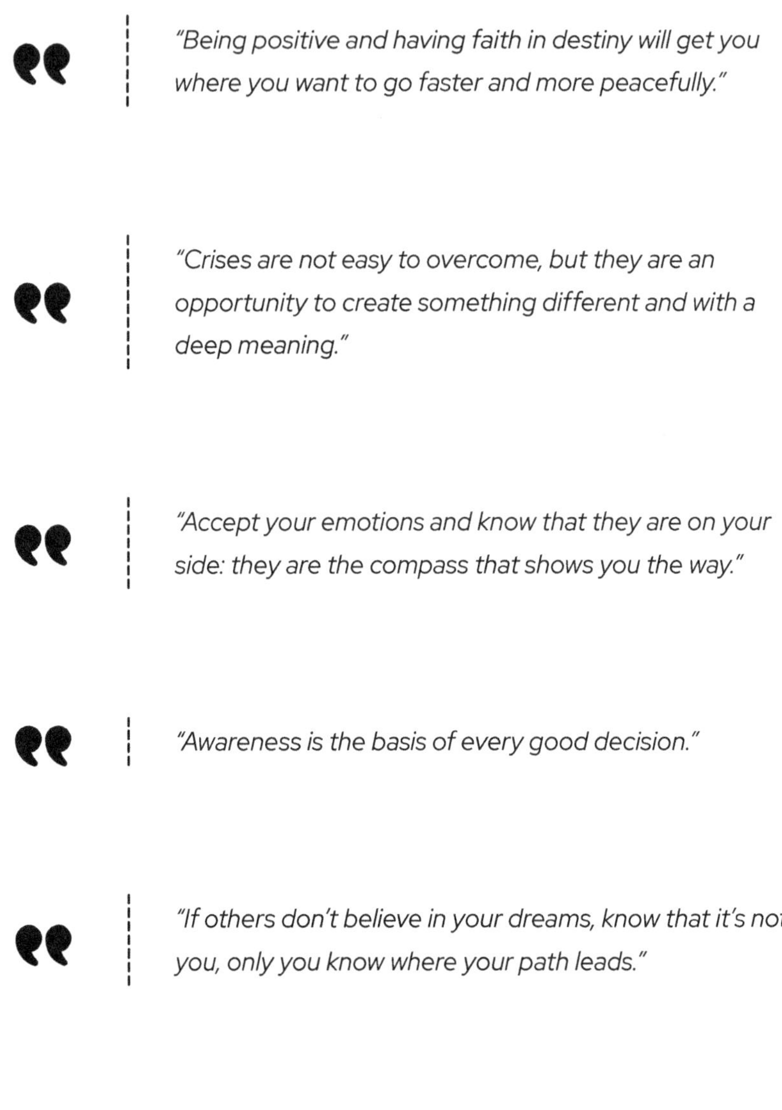

"Being positive and having faith in destiny will get you where you want to go faster and more peacefully."

"Crises are not easy to overcome, but they are an opportunity to create something different and with a deep meaning."

"Accept your emotions and know that they are on your side: they are the compass that shows you the way."

"Awareness is the basis of every good decision."

"If others don't believe in your dreams, know that it's not you, only you know where your path leads."

"Listen to everyone but follow yourself."

"Be aware of your talents and use them every day doing your best, you'll be surprised how much it comes back to you."

"Every time you recognize a demotivating or unhelpful belief, brush it away and repeat only phrases that strengthen your mind."

"Patience is the virtue of the strongest."

"Don't wait for others to make you happy, start making yourself happy."

"Don't compare yourself to others as it only leads to frustration. You are you and you have your story, start there."

"If you feel something is good for you, fight for it."

"Gratitude is like magic that produces joy in your heart."

"There is a time to fight and a time to let go. Go with the flow, there is often wisdom inside."

"Follow the wave to the rhythm of the wind."

"Remember to be as generous and good to yourself as you are to others."

"Smile because smiling opens a thousand doors."

"Happiness is a state of mind."

"Happy and successful people believe in themselves unconditionally. Always believe that you can do it."

"The opinion of others has a profound value, but it is one opinion among many. Value yours more than theirs, you know your heart best!"

"Don't let anyone make you doubt yourself and your possibilities, you can do it!"

"Happiness is leaving aside what you really don't need."

"Don't pretend to be perfect, what you have to expect is to do your best."

"Free yourself from the judgment of others and you will begin to fly lightly."

"Dream because dreams are the fuel of life."

"Always have faith and you will move mountains."

"Let yourself be guided by your values, not by what others say."

"There are no mistakes but feedback and lessons to learn."

"If you turn defeats into opportunities, you will always win."

"Big changes start with small steps."

"You always have the option to choose even when it doesn't seem like it."

We can always change for the better and start now!

21

Start Now

You have reached the end of this journey. You did it! Now remember that there is always the possibility to start. There is not a special day in the calendar. No Christmas, or new year's Ave or Birthday ... There is only one decision that can keep you away from a better life. This decision is simply your decision. You can always start, even sometimes it does not feel like this. That is the bad and good news: it depends on you.

So remember: Start now, and you can decide when it is "your now". The task of today is simply the following: cut the "post it" below and place it where you can always see it.

If you like today, simply cut the following "post it" in place it in a place you can always see it. It is your personal reminder. It shows you that you have power, you can do it, you have a value and there is hope for everything. We can always #changeforthebetter.

Notes about the author

Moira Buzzolani is a transformation and change leader and a DYL certified coach with a diverse background spanning various industries and organizations. With a keen focus on individuals, teams, and organizations, she is dedicated to helping them develop creativity and navigate through changes in a positive way.

Having lived in both Italy and Germany and having worked internationally for over a decade, Moira has brought innovation and creative perspectives to numerous sectors. She firmly believes in the power of people as the key driver of success and considers the ability to reinvent oneself as a vital skill in every aspect of life, whether personal or professional.

Moira holds the conviction that creativity and adaptability are the essential ingredients for future success, and she continually emphasizes their importance. With her expertise and unwavering commitment, she strives to empower others to unlock their potential and achieve their goals.

Acknowledgement

I would like to thank all the people who, in various ways, have contributed to the creation of this "workbook". I am grateful for the feedback received and for the ideas that experts, friends, or acquaintances have been willing to share with me. Thank you all.

In specific, David, Christian, Fiorella, Chiara, Eleonora, Cinzia, Natsuko, Sigrid, Kate, Diego, Giulia, Alessandro.

This "working book" represents an "ongoing project". If you have any feedback or ideas on how to improve it, or if you simply want to let me know what you particularly liked, please contact me at www.moirabuzzolani.com

Recommended readings

- ▸ The coaching habit: say less, ask more and change the way you lead forever, B. Stanier Michael;

- ▸ Designing your life, Bill Burnett & Dave Evans;

- ▸ Designing your work life, Bill Burnett & Dave Evans;

- ▸ Start with why, Simon Sinek;

- ▸ Be a Leader, Daniel Goleman, Richard E. Boyatzis, Annie McKee;

- ▸ The subtle art of not giving a f*ck, Mark Manson;

- ▸ The art of happiness, The Dalai Lama;

- ▸ Ho'oponoponomo, Ulrich Duprée;

- ▸ Ikigai: the japanese secret to a long and happy life, Hector Garcia and Francesco Mirales;

- ▸ The luck factor, Richard Wiseman;

- ▸ The happiness code, Dominique Bertolucci;

- ▸ The 5 seconds rule: Mel Robbins;

For more book's suggestions please follow me on Instagram:
mbuzz_consultingcoaching

Notes

What message do you want to take with you after reading this book? Write it here:

Draw here a symbol that reminds you of your personal journey and that it is never too late to start a new positive chapter in your life.